29-6-99

To Alec,

Hope you have a great 40th
birthday. Lots of love,

Jean

x.

Crikey I'm...

40

Crikey I'm...™

40

Contributors

Dr David Haslam
Victoria Warner
Eliza Williams

Edited by

Steve Hare

Cover Illustration by

Ian Pollock

PURPLE HOUSE

Published by Purple House Limited 1998
75 Banbury Road
Oxford OX2 6PE

© Purple House Limited 1998

Cover illustration: © Ian Pollock/The Inkshed

Crikey I'm... is a trademark of Purple House
Limited

A catalogue record for this book is available
from the British Library

ISBN 1-84118-013-0

Printed in Great Britain by
Cox and Wyman

Acknowledgements

We are grateful to everyone who helped in
the compilation of this book, particularly to
the following:

Stephen Franks of Franks and Franks (Design)

Inform Group Worldwide (Reproduction)

Dave Kent of the Kobal Collection

Office of National Statistics

Bodleian Library, Oxford

Central Library, Oxford

British Film Institute

Liz Brown

Mark McClintock

Hannah Wren

Illustrations

Contents

Crikey, I'm 40!

So – today is my fortieth birthday. Things have been building up to this for some time now. Forty years. Fourteen thousand six hundred days, give or take a few leap years. Three hundred and fifty thousand four hundred hours. Twenty-one million minutes and then some. So who's counting, anyway?

Forty.

40.

XL.

The big Four-Oh.

Uh oh. People are going to be telling me I'm over the hill. Other people, usually those who've already been there, done that, will regale me with stuff about life beginning. Age seems to bring a more understanding attitude towards clichés.

If I am lucky I shall receive some birthday cards that are larger than is strictly necessary, with jokes as old as I am beginning to feel and ghastly cartoons depicting golf or fishing.

If I am extremely unlucky, total strangers approaching suburban roundabouts will be informed of my new status by prominent and garish signs.

Why all this fuss about 40? What have I still got left to look forward to? Do I now spend more time looking back? Are we talking bedroom slippers and cocoa?

This is not, however, the end of life as you know it and the start of your decline into senility. Statistically, you are scarcely in your middle age. You have several decades of full and active life ahead, to be explored and enjoyed to the full.

Your fortieth birthday is the ideal occasion to declare to the world that you're not yet ready to let yourself go to seed.

This book aims to help you on this new journey of discovery: to welcome the future with open arms, while celebrating the 40 full years you've already enjoyed.

Sean Connery and Ursula Andress starred in the first James Bond film, *Doctor No*, released in 1962.

Famous Contemporaries

Björn Borg, tennis player, born 6/6/56
Sebastian Coe, athlete, born 29/9/56
Bernard Sumner, musician, born 4/1/56
Paul Merton, comedian, born 17/1/57
Danny Baker, entertainer, born 22/6/57
Dawn French, comedian, born 11/10/57
Julian Cope, musician, born 21/10/57
Glenn Hoddle, football player/manager, born 27/10/57
Daley Thompson, athlete, born 30/7/58
Madonna, pop star, born 16/8/58
Michael Jackson, pop star, born 29/8/58
Jools Holland, musician and TV presenter, born 24/1/58
Rik Mayall, comedian, born 7/3/58
Sharon Stone, actor, born 10/3/58
Holly Hunter, actor, born 20/3/58
Gary Oldman, actor and director, born 21/3/58
Michelle Pfeiffer, actor, born 29/4/58
Paul Weller, musician, born 25/5/58
Lenny Henry, comedian, born 29/5/58
John McEnroe, tennis player, born 16/2/59
Emma Thompson, actor, born 15/4/59
Martin Brundle, racing driver, born 1/6/59
Kevin Spacey, actor, born 26/7/59
Prince Andrew, born 19/2/60
Linford Christie, athlete, born 2/4/60
Hugh Grant, actor, born 9/9/60
Bono, musician, born 10/5/60
Gary Lineker, footballer/presenter, born 30/11/60
Kenneth Branagh, actor and director, born 10/12/60
Jim Carrey, actor, born 17/1/62
Tom Cruise, actor, born 3/7/62
Demi Moore, actor, born 11/11/62
Jodie Foster, actor, born 19/11/62

Are You a Reincarnation of...?

Dame Christabel Pankhurst, British suffragette, died 14/3/58

Ralph Vaughan Williams, composer, died 26/8/58

Tyrone Power, actor, died 15/11/58

Buddy Holly, singer, died 3/2/59

Lou Costello, comedian, died 3/3/59

Raymond Chandler, author, died 26/3/59

Frank Lloyd Wright, architect, died 9/4/59

Billie Holliday, singer, died 17/7/59

Sir Jacob Epstein, sculptor, died 19/8/59

Errol Flynn, actor, died 14/10/59

Albert Camus, author, died 4/1/60

Nevil Shute, author, died 12/1/60

Boris Pasternak, author, died 30/5/60

Aneurin 'Nye' Bevan, British statesman, died 6/7/60

Clark Gable, actor, died 16/11/60

Oscar Hammerstein, musician, died 23/8/60

George Formby, comedian, died 6/3/61

Gary Cooper, actor, died 13/5/61

Carl Gustav Jung, psychoanalyst, died 6/6/61

Ernest Hemingway, author, died 2/7/61

Victoria Sackville-West, author, died 2/6/62

William Faulkner, author, died 6/7/62

Marilyn Monroe, actor and icon, died 5/8/62

Charles Laughton, actor and director, died 15/12/62

The first logos for Tyne Tees and Anglia Television.

6

Forty Years On

So you're forty. What does it mean? What have you lived through? You were born into the era of Harold Wilson's 'white heat of technology', which, it must be admitted, was still fairly luke-warm compared to the fax machines, mobile phones, personal computers, VCRs, smart bombs and the internet we all take for granted these days.

The tail end of the fifties and early sixties saw the last few regions around Britain – Tyne Tees, Ulster and Anglia, and

You will have blinked an average of 220 million times by the age of 40.

finally Westward Television and the Wales Television Association, the fifteenth and last independent television station – bringing black and white commercial TV on 405-line transmission to the whole country. There was already talk of changing to 625 lines, issuing a licence for a third channel, and the possibility of colour TV. This latter was a reality, by 1962, only in the United States, Japan and, perhaps surprisingly, Cuba. All the same, when a 1959 TV thriller *When the Sun Goes Down* was prefaced by an 'urgent announcement' concerning a 'new and terrifying satellite hanging over London', people fainted or dashed into the street in terror, just as Orson Welles' radio audience had done years earlier.

Television ownership was growing by one million a year; cinema audiences were falling just as fast.

Attendances for 1961 stood at just one third of those for 1948. Over the same period some 1,700 cinemas closed, converting to bowling alleys, bingo halls and supermarkets. The 3,000 left operating relied more and more on big budget spectaculars: *Ben-Hur*, the most costly film ever made, at five million dollars in 1959, *El Cid*, *Spartacus*, *The Alamo*. British films of the time dealt with slightly more contemporary issues: gritty realism was the order of the day with *Room at the Top*, *Look Back in Anger*, *Saturday Night and Sunday Morning*, *A Taste of Honey*. It was also the time of landmark thrillers and comedies: *Psycho* and *Some Like it Hot*. For beatniks and intellectuals there were significant continental contributions: *A Bout de Souffle*, *Ashes and Diamonds*, *Tirez sur le Pianiste*, *La Dolce Vita*, *Hiroshima mon Amour*.

1959 saw the space race hot up, with six Russian and American satellites orbiting the earth, and the first photographs taken of the dark side of the moon. By the early sixties there would be assorted animals and plants launched into orbit, and ultimately men: Major Gagarin and Alan Shepard. On earth, Christopher

On an average week, 40 year-olds spend 60 hours asleep; 33 hours on free time; 30 hours in paid work; 24 hours in domestic work; 17 hours in personal care and 4 hours in household maintenance. They have an average of 4 hours' free time on a weekday and 6 hours of free time on a weekend day.

Cockerell tested the first hovercraft. The search for a cure for the common cold continued, and further research determined the links between 'hard', saturated fats and coronary disease, and heavy smoking and lung cancer.

> **'Women over 40 are at their best, but men over 30 are too old to recognise it.'**
> Jean-Paul Belmondo.

Yet amid all this ancient history, there is much that remains familiar, and carries distinct recent echoes. Iraq in 1959 was 'a most unhappy, distracted and misgoverned country', pressing claims for Kuwait as part of its territory. Labour lost their third election on the trot in the same year. In the inevitable post mortems that followed, it was felt that in this prosperous nation people no longer wanted to think of themselves as 'working class'. The party name was called in question, with suggestions of 'Labour and Radical' and 'Labour and Reform' suggested. 'Labour and Socialist' was not seriously touted, any more than 'New Labour'.

Macmillan remained Prime Minister, with Edward Heath as Minister of Labour and Ernest Marples, who had previously introduced Ernie and Premium Bonds to Britain, as Minister of Transport. His concerns

> **29% of 40 year-olds have tried an illegal drug.**

a Mars a day helps you work, rest and play

Because Mars contains:
GLUCOSE & SUGAR to give you energy while you work
MILK to nourish you while you relax
CHOCOLATE to keep you going while you play

Mars give you energy in 1960.

now were largely with the introduction of seat belts and parking meters, and the expansion of the road network. In November 1959 he officially opened a 55-mile stretch of dual carriageway from Luton to Dunchurch, the first section of the M1 motorway, where he was reported as being appalled by the 'speed and badness' of the driving he had witnessed. A hand-painted slogan 'Marples Must Go' was still visible on this very section well into the eighties.

While roads prospered, the railways were subject to Dr Beeching's report, leading to the closure of over 1,000 stations and branch lines around the country, despite the fact that by 1960 the number of miles run by diesel and electric trains finally overtook those run under steam power.

After several abortive attempts, a plan was finally agreed for the development of the Barbican area of the City of London. And the growing prolifera-tion of tall buildings in

By the time you reach 40, you will have exper-ienced an average of 1.47 billion heart beats.

London led the GPO to announce that they would replace existing radio masts with a futuristic 500-foot tower, incorporating public viewing platforms and a revolving restaurant. Plans were hatched for the National Theatre to be built on the South Bank of the Thames; the Bull Ring in Birmingham; the destruc-tion of inner city areas everywhere to make way for urban motorways; and a road bridge over the Severn, to be funded by tolls. And to the fury of many, the magnificent Doric Arch, gateway to Euston Station, was demolished during the station's redevelopment.

> 'Women are most fascinating between the ages of 35 and 40, after they have won a few races and know how to pace themselves. Since few women ever pass 40, maximum fascination can continue indefinitely'
> Christian Dior.

It was the era of new towns – Crawley, Hemel Hempstead, Skelmersdale; the expansion of Bracknell and Basingtoke; atomic power stations were springing up around the coasts. Cars over ten years old were now obliged to undergo a test for roadworthiness. It was the era of art thefts, including Goya's portrait of the Duke of Wellington, only days after it was acquired by the National Gallery. It was the era of spies, with George Blake sentenced to 42 years; and Nazi hunting, with Adolf Eichmann snatched from Argentina to Israel, where he stood trial in a bullet-proof glass case, to be hanged in 1962.

Teddy bears remained popular toys, with the latest versions in rayon and stuffed with foam rubber which could be washed and 'put through the mangle'. Dolls, on the other hand, 'now come dressed to current fashion, Gina Lollabrigida hair-dos, emphasised bosoms, high-heeled shoes and short skirts'.

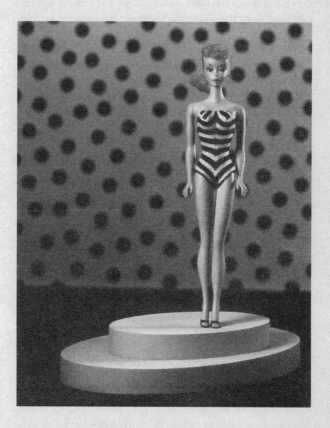

Barbie strikes a pose in 1958.

There was talk of drive-in banks and electronic accounting. Customers could now have their names printed on individual cheques and paying-in slips.

The Manchester Guardian became just *The Guardian*. The last tram ran in Sheffield in 1960 and on 1 January 1961, the farthing ceased to be legal tender.

Bernard Miles opened the first new theatre in the City precincts for 300 years, The Mermaid. Along with *Salad Days, West Side Story* and *My Fair Lady,*

40 year-olds watch an average of 26.2 hours of television per week.

The Mousetrap was remarkable for the fact that it ran throughout the year 1959. The Common Market was known as The Six – France, West Germany, Italy and the Benelux countries. Britain, against the increasing hostility of de Gaulle, had to content themselves for the time being with membership of the European Free Trade Association.

Amidst this antipathy, the Channel Tunnel Study Group reported in April 1960. Having examined the possibility of road or rail tunnels or a bridge, they decided the tunnel should carry

By the age of 40, you will have grown an average of 15 metres of finger nails.

a railway, 'on account of greater profitability'. The

estimated cost of construction was £130 million. And by the end of 1961 it was almost certain that Britain and France would co-operate on the development of a supersonic airliner.

Britain had further problems in the Commonwealth, particularly in South Africa where Macmillan detected a 'wind of change'. That came at Sharpeville, where panicking police turned automatic weapons on demonstrators, killing 69 Africans and wounding nearly 200 others. The Reverend David Sheppard refused to play in Test Matches against the country when it toured Britain. South Africa was soon to split from the Commonwealth.

> **40 year-olds spend an average of £2.40 on the National Lottery per week.**

Britons did not only demonstrate against apartheid. CND held regular Easter marches to Aldermaston. Some 100,000 turned up to follow and listen to Michael Foot and A.J.P. Taylor in 1960. 'For the first time since the days of the militant suffragettes', reported *The Economist*, 'a group of people in this country are actively seeking to be sent to prison as a means of political protest.' Those so inclined included the 89 year-old 'ageing adolescent', Bertrand Russell, sentenced to seven days in 1961 for protesting against nuclear proliferation.

Coke target the sixties youth.

This threat was very real, with tension building up between Russia's ageing leader, Khruschev, and the United States' youngest President, John F. Kennedy. Cuba, recently liberated by 'the bearded guerrilla leader' Dr Fidel Castro from the corrupt Batistà régime, promptly nationalised American interests, and sought succour and weaponry from the Eastern bloc. The CIA funded a farcical invasion by Cuban exiles at the Bahia de Cochinos. 1962 would see the near disaster of the Cuban missile crisis.

> **'At 20 years of age, the will reigns; at 30, the wit; and at 40, the judgement.'**
> Benjamin Franklin, *Poor Richard's Almanac*, 1758.

East Germans were leaving their country at the rate of 4,000 a week in 1961, when the border was sealed, and a substantial wall dividing Berlin was erected. At the same time Russia was pointedly testing nuclear devices, and Kennedy announced huge additional defence appropriations.

North Vietnamese guerrillas were threatening to overrun the pro-Western South. America, fearing a domino

> **You will have produced an average of 21,000 litres of urine by the age of 40.**

effect that would see Laos, Cambodia and possibly Thailand go the same way, began to ship helicopters

17

and training aircraft over, along with some 400 service personnel.

At the age of 40, you will have worked continuously for 3.7 years.

Against this background of international turmoil, Britain was thriving. Unemployment fell to 421,000 by the start of the sixties, with over 251,000 unfilled vacancies. This, by any definition, was full employment. Commonwealth immigration was encouraged to help fill unpopular vacancies. The standard rate of income tax fell to 7/9d in the pound (around 39 per cent). The bank rate was four per cent.

The Obscene Publications Act was tested in October 1960 by Penguin's proposal to publish the first unexpurgated edition of *Lady Chatterley's Lover*. After a sensational court case, the book was cleared, and some 200,000 copies sold out immediately at 3/6 a copy. Sales of the book were only overtaken in 1961, when Cambridge and Oxford University Press published The New English Bible, which sold some 2.5 million copies in 1961. But by then, the sixties, and all that they would come to stand for, was under way.

'We don't understand life any better at 40 than at 20, but we know it and admit it.'
Jules Renard

Slade's *Mama Weer All Crazee Now* reached Number One in 1972.

LADY LOVERLEY'S CHATTER

THIS IS THE

ABRIDGED

CENSORED

EXPURGATED

INCOMPLETE

EDITION

CAN BE IMPORTED AND IMPRISON

Lady Loverley's Chatter, published in 1960, mocks the *Lady Chatterley's Lover* scandal.

What Happened When

A Brief Review of the Last Forty Years

1960

- John F. Kennedy becomes US president.
- *Coronation Street* is first broadcast by Granada.

1961

- The oral contraceptive pill becomes available in the UK.
- USSR launch the first man, Yuri Gagarin, into space.
- The East/West German border is closed and the Berlin Wall is erected, causing outrage in the West.
- *Catch-22* by Joseph Heller is published.

1962

- Marilyn Monroe is found dead in an apparent suicide.
- Andy Warhol's Campbell's Soup Cans are exhibited in New York.

1963

- Kennedy is assassinated in Dallas, allegedly by Lee Harvey Oswald, who is later shot by Jack Rubenstein (Jack Ruby).
- Beatlemania grips Britain.
- Weight Watchers is founded in New York.

1964

- Cassius Clay becomes heavyweight world champion aged 22 after beating Sonny Liston as the 7–1 underdog.
- Nelson Mandela is sentenced to life imprisonment in South Africa for 'treason'.

• The United States goes to war against the North Vietnamese communists.

1965

• Malcolm X is shot dead during a speech to his followers in New York.

• Ian Brady and Myra Hindley are arrested for the murder of Lesley Ann Downing and police search for more bodies thought to be buried on the Saddleworth Moor.

• The death penalty is abolished in Britain.

1966

• London is officially 'swinging'.

• England win the World Cup, beating Germany 4–2.

• Barclays Bank introduce Britain's first credit card, the Barclaycard.

• A slag heap in Aberfan, South Wales, collapses and buries the local school, killing 116 children and 28 adults.

1967

• Protests against the war in Vietnam in the US and Europe.

• The Abortion Act legalises abortion in Britain.

• Israel wins the Six Day War against the Arabs, extending Israeli territory by more than twice its original size.

• The first human heart transplant is performed on Louis Washkansky in South Africa, by Dr Christiaan Barnard. He survives for 18 days.

1968

• Martin Luther King is shot dead in Memphis.

• Street battles occur in Londonderry, Northern Ireland,

THE SUNDAY TIMES COLOUR SECTION

A sharp glance at the mood of Britain

and a new James Bond story by Ian Fleming

The Sunday Times introduce their first colour supplement in 1962.

following the police break-up of a demonstration by Catholics against discrimination in housing and employment.
• 13 members of the cast of *Hair* appear naked on stage after play censorship is lifted.

1969

• A human egg is fertilised in a test tube for the first time in Britain.
• US astronauts, Neil Armstrong and Edwin 'Buzz' Aldrin land on the moon.
• Sharon Tate and four others are murdered by Charles Manson's cult 'family'.
• Half a million people attend the first free rock festival, held for 3 days in Woodstock, US.
• *Monty Python's Flying Circus* begins broadcasting.

1970s

1970

• The age of adulthood is reduced in Britain from 21 to 18.
• Schools in Britain switch from a selective to a comprehensive system.
• The Gay Liberation Front is formed.

1971

• The first British soldier is killed in Ulster since troops entered in 1969.
• Jim Morrison is found dead in his bath in Paris.
• *The Godfather* (directed by Francis Ford Coppola) is released.

1972

• Miners' strikes over pay claims cause blackouts across Britain. Householders are asked to only heat one room and industry is officially working a three-day week.

• Nixon aides are arrested for trying to bug the Democrat headquarters in the Watergate complex in the run up to the presidential elections. Nixon denies any responsibility and is re-elected.

• The Race Relations Act comes into force in Britain – employers can not discriminate on the grounds of colour.

1973

• Britain officially joins the EEC.

• The oil states rise the price of oil in the western world as a response to US intervention in the Yom Kippur war in the Middle East.

• 'Glam rock' is popular, featuring artists such as Gary Glitter, T-Rex and Elton John.

1974

• Nixon resigns after admitting participation in the Watergate scandal. He is the first US President to resign.

• Britain's first McDonald's opens in Woolwich.

• Lord Lucan disappears after allegedly murdering his nanny and attacking his estranged wife.

1975

• The war in Vietnam is over as Saigon is taken by the North Vietnamese and all US troops are withdrawn.

• Bill Gates, aged 19, and a friend form the Microsoft computer company.

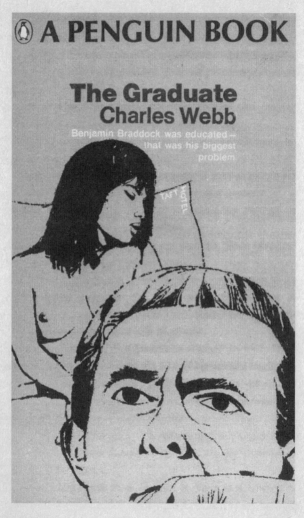

The Graduate, published in 1963, led to the classic sixties film.

1976

• 14 year-old Nadia Comaneci of Romania is the first person to win a maximum 10 score in Olympic women's gymnastics.

1977

• 25 years of the Queen's reign are celebrated by a week of Silver Jubilee celebrations in the summer.

• Two homosexual men die and are thought to be the first AIDS (Acquired Immune Deficiency Syndrome) victims in New York, following diagnosis of rare cancer Karposi's sarcoma.

• Punk music is prominent, and projects The Sex Pistols, The Clash, and Iggy Pop to fame.

1978

• Sid Vicious is charged with murdering his girlfriend Nancy Spungen in New York. He dies of a heroin overdose less than four months later.

1979

• Vietnamese forces seize control of Cambodia, overthrowing the Khmer Rouge. Pol Pot's killing fields are discovered – it is believed that 3–4 million have been murdered or starved to death under his regime.

• Margaret Thatcher becomes the first woman British Prime Minister.

1980s

1980

• Drought and war leads to ten million people facing famine in East Africa.

- John Lennon is shot dead outside his apartment building in New York by obsessive fan Mark Chapman.
- Sebastian Coe wins gold in the 1,500 metres and Steve Ovett takes gold in the 800 metres Moscow.

1981
- Ten IRA hunger strikers die in the Maze prison, protesting for the right to be segregated from Loyalist supporters in jail.
- Riots and looting break out in Brixton and across the country owing to racial tension, unemployment and poor housing.
- Prince Charles and Lady Diana Spencer marry, watched by 700 million television viewers worldwide.

1982
- Argentina invade and capture the Falkland Islands but are defeated by the British troops after a two-month war.
- The first compact discs are released by Philips.

1983
- Reagan proposes a 'a Star Wars' defence system, consisting of a missile shield in space across the US to protect it from Russian attack.
- The pound coin comes into circulation.

1984
- Jayne Torvill and Christopher Dean win Olympic gold for their ice dancing to Ravel's *Bolero*.
- A nationwide miners' strike, led by Arthur Scargill, follows low pay increases and the beginning of pit closures.
- An IRA bomb blasts the Tory conference HQ in Brighton killing four people but narrowly missing Margaret Thatcher.

Rod Stewart's classic 1971 album, *Every Picture Tells A Story*.

• A group of international singers form Band Aid and release *Do They Know It's Christmas* to raise money to help the famine victims in Africa.

1985

• Football violence instigated by British fans occurs across Britain and Europe. A fire in the main stand of Bradford City football ground kills over 40 fans. Over 40 Britons and Italians are killed when a safety wall collapses in Brussels' Heysel Stadium.

1986

• Argentina beat Belguim 3–2 in the World Cup. They knock England out in the quarter-finals with help from Maradona's 'hand of God'.

1987

• 187 die as *The Herald of Free Enterprise* ferry sinks leaving Zeebrugge when the bow doors are not shut properly.
• Stock market falls by 10% on 'Black Monday' causing the worst crash this century.
• 6,000 emergency calls are made to the Fire Brigade in 24 hours due to the worst storm this century in England.
• 30 die in a fire at King's Cross tube station.
• Reagan and Gorbachev sign a mutual agreement to cut the size of their nuclear weapons.

1988

• Pan Am flight 103 from London to New York crashes in Lockerbie, Scotland killing all aboard.
• *A Brief History of Time* by Stephen Hawking is published.

1989

• 94 fans die in the Hillsborough stadium disaster in Sheffield after fans are crushed when too many are let in.

• Tanks roll into Tiananmen Square in China and crush pro-democracy attempts, killing more than 2,000 people.

• 'The Guildford Four' are released from jail after serving 14 years for wrongful convictions of IRA bombing attacks on pubs in Guildford in 1974.

• The Berlin Wall is pulled down, symbolising the end of Soviet international communism.

• Acid House rave parties in the open air attract thousands of young people, despite clampdowns by police.

1990s

1990

• The government gives £2.2 million for research into BSE, known as 'mad cow disease'.

• Thatcher resigns as British PM to be replaced by John Major.

1991

• The Gulf war begins after Iraqi troops refuse to withdraw from Kuwait by the deadline given by the UN.

• The 'Birmingham Six' are released from jail.

• Apartheid collapses in South Africa.

• Civil war breaks out in Yugoslavia between Serbs, Croats and Muslims.

• Terry Waite, the last British hostage, is freed after being held in Beirut for five years.

1992
• Windsor Castle is badly damaged by fire.

1993
• Two ten year-old boys are arrested and found guilty for the murder of toddler James Bulger.
• The European Union is formed with the implementation of the Maastricht treaty.
• *Schindler's List* (directed by Steven Spielberg) is released.

1994
• Frederick and Rosemary West are charged with the murder of eight women found buried in the garden of their house.
• Following the sudden death of John Smith, Tony Blair becomes the leader of the Labour party.
• The Channel Tunnel opens between Britain and France.
• Nelson Mandela is inaugurated as South Africa's first black President.
• O. J. Simpson leads police cars and TV reporters on a car chase across Los Angeles after failing to appear for an arraignment on charges of murdering his former wife Nicole and her friend Ronald Goldman.
• £7 million is spent on the first day of UK Lottery sales.

1995
• O. J. Simpson is found not guilty of murder.
• Princess Diana gives a television interview on *Panorama* revealing her affair with James Hewitt and her feelings towards her marriage.
• The rise of 'Brit pop', with chart wars between Blur, Oasis, Pulp, Supergrass...

The Selfish Gene, the commercially-successful science book, published in 1976.

Forty Grand National Winners

1959 Mr J. E. Bigg's Oxo, ridden by M Scudamore.
1960 Miss W. H. S. Wallace's Merryman II, ridden by G. Scott.
1961 Mr C. Vaughan's Nicolaus Silver, ridden by H. Beesley.
1962 Mr N. Cohen's Kilmore, ridden by F. Winter.
1963 Mr P. B. Raymond's Ayala, ridden by P. Buckley.
1964 Mr J. Goodman's Team Spirit, ridden by G. W. Robinson.
1965 Mrs M. Stephenson's Jay Trump, ridden by M. C. Smith.
1966 Mr S. Levy's Anglo, ridden by T. Norman.
1967 Mr C. P. T. Watkins' Foinavon, ridden by J. Buckingham.
1968 Mr J. Manners' Red Alligator, ridden by B. Fletcher.
1969 Mr T. H. McKoy's Highland Wedding, ridden by E. Harty.
1970 Mr A. Chambers' Gay Trip, ridden by P. Taaffe.
1971 Mr F Pontin's Specify, ridden by J. Cook.
1972 Capt. T. Forster's Well To Do, ridden by G. Thorner.
1973 Mr N. Le Mare's Red Rum, ridden by B. Fletcher.
1974 Mr N. Le Mare's Red Rum, ridden by B. Fletcher.
1975 Mr R. Guest's L'Escargot, ridden by T. Carberry.
1976 Mr P. B. Raymond's Rag Trade, ridden by J. Burke.
1977 Mr N. Le Mare's Red Rum, ridden by T. Stack.
1978 Mrs D. Whitaker's Lucius, ridden by B. R. Davies.
1979 Mr J. Douglas' Rubstic, ridden by M. Barnes.
1980 Mr R. C. Stewart's Ben Nevis, ridden by C. Fenwick.
1981 Mr S. Embiricos' Aldaniti, ridden by R. Champion.
1982 Mr F. Gilman's Grittar, ridden by C. Saunders.
1983 Mr B. M. H. Burrough's Corbiere, ridden by B. de Haan.
1984 Mr. Richard Shaw's Hallo Dandy, ridden by N. Doughty.
1985 Duchess of Westminster's Last Suspect, ridden by H. Davies.
1986 Mr P. Luff's West Tip, ridden by R. Dunwoody.
1987 Mr H. J. Joel's Maori Venture, ridden by S. C. Knight.
1988 Miss J. Reed's Rhyme 'n' Reason, ridden by B. Powell.
1989 Mr E. Harvey's Little Polveir, ridden by J. Frost.
1990 Mrs H. Duffey's Mr Frisk, ridden by M. Armytage.
1991 Sir Eric Parker's Seagram, ridden by N. Hawke.
1992 Mrs D. Thompson's Party Politics, ridden by C. Llewellyn.
1993 Race declared void after two false starts.
1994 Mr Freddie Starr's Miinnehoma, ridden by R. Dunwoody.
1995 Messrs G. & C Johnson's Royal Athlete, ridden by J. Titley.
1996 Mr A. Wate's Rough Quest, ridden by M. A. Fitzgerald.
1997 Mr S. Clarke's Lord Gyllene, ridden by T. Dobbin.
1998 The Summit Partnership's Earth Summit, ridden by C. Llewellyn.

The Middle Ages

Forty Then and Now

Most people would say that when you turn 40, you enter into the misty realms of something called 'middle age' (or mature adulthood, to be more politically correct). Perhaps we are wrong to attach a stigma to the phrase: after all, 'middle age' surely implies that you still have half your life ahead, which is, statistically speaking, quite true.

Turning 40 has not always been synonymous with middle age, however: alarmingly enough, back in the seventeenth century, a fortieth birthday would almost certainly be seen as an indication of old age. After all, average life expectancy back then bottomed out at around 20 years. Even during the last century, things weren't looking good for a 40 year-old: many of your

---

Forty in the Bible

- Moses spent 40 days and nights on Mount Sinai.
- There are 40 days in Lent, because Jesus spent 40 days and nights in the wilderness.
- The Great Flood lasted for 40 days and nights.
- Elijah was fed by ravens for 40 days and nights.
- The Jews wandered in the desert for 40 years.
- According to the Bible, a mother is unclean for 40 days after giving birth to a boy and for 80 days after giving birth to a girl.

The reason for this significance is likely to be because the early meaning of the word 'forty' was simply 'lots', and it could well have been used to indicate this in the Bible.

---

contemporaries would have popped off some ten years previously, and you yourself would only have another three years or so left before the Grim Reaper should come to collect you at the tender age of 43. Amazingly, such low life expectancy rates are not entirely a thing of the past: in Sierra Leone, owing to factors like poor nutrition and civil war, you can expect to live, on average, a mere 40 years.

By the age of 40, you will have spent an average of 1.9 years eating.

In the fourteenth century, reaching the grand old age of 40 was even more of an achievement – especially with the ever-increasing outbreaks of bubonic plague. Top of the range for infectiousness and sheer epidemic potential, the Black Death carried off many 40 year-olds in their prime. Symptoms were hard to miss: the hard swellings, black pustules and vomiting of blood normally gave it away. It was absolutely the only plague for those busy people with no spare time in which to sicken and die: the whole process of infection and death could happen within a mere 24 hours. If, as a busy 40 year-old, you craved a quiet life (and death), then leprosy was probably the disease for you. After being pronounced officially dead by the church, you were cast out and may well have ended up in a leper hospital, or lazar house. Here sufferers lived in splendid isolation, often self-sufficient, farming land or keeping pigs. The disease, of course, was incurable: although this didn't prevent well-meaning attempts at remedies which included a concoction made from leeks and adders as one of the more appetising ones.

As a seventeenth-century 40 year-old, chances were you would be married, although for women any reproductive life would be more or less over. Back then, your fertile years were very much curtailed: owing to poor nutrition and living standards, puberty didn't begin until 16, and the menopause would kick in at about or before 40. Just as well, really, because with a distinct lack of effective contraception you'd probably have spent a large part of your life pregnant. As a working-class parent, most of your children would have left home already at the tender age of 13 to work, although 'retirement' was still a very long way off for you, and unfortunately, would probably coincide rather neatly with your death.

> The Babylonians considered 40 to be an extremely significant figure, because one of the star constellations – the Pleiades, or Seven Sisters – disappeared from the sky for 40 nights each year. This coincides with the rainy season, and the reappearance of the constellation marked the end of the season, which is when the Babylonians celebrated New Year.

Suddenly 'middle age' doesn't seem like quite such a bad thing!

Carol Ward with Jemima in BBC television's *Play School*.

Do You Remember...?

Blasts From The Past

Children's TV from the 1960s

Play School – featuring Humpty, Jemima, Hamble, Big Ted, Little Ted and Dapple the Rocking Horse, the useful box and various shaped windows:

> Here is a house,
> Here is a door,
> Windows one, two, three and four,
> Ready to knock, turn the lock,
> It's Play School

When it first began, there were two budgerigars, two mice (Henry and Henrietta), one rabbit (George) and two goldfish.

Play Away – presenters included Brian Cant and Jeremy Irons.

Blue Peter – favourite phrases included 'Here's one I made earlier'; 'double-sided stickytape'; 'sticky-backed plastic'.

In 1969, Lulu the elephant disgraced herself on the show...

Tales of the Riverbank

The Magic Roundabout – featured Dylan, Zebedee, Dougal, Brian the Snail, and Ermintrude.

Jackanory – favourite readers included Sir Compton Mackenzie, Edward Ardizzone, Eileen Cowell, Bernard Cribbens and Kenneth Williams.

Top of the Form

The Clangers

Trumpton – featuring Pugh, Pugh, Barney McGrew, Cuthbert, Dibble and Grubb:

> Here is the clock, the Trumpton clock
> Telling the time steadily, sensibly,
> Never too quickly, never too slowly
> Telling the time for Trumpton

How – presented by Bunty James, Fred Dinenage, Jack Hargreaves and Jon Miller. They always greeted the audience with an American Indian-style 'How'.

Crackerjack – with the Crackerjack pencil as consolation prize. First presented by Eamonn Andrews, Pete Glazer and Leslie Crowther.

Animal Magic – featuring Johnny Morris as the zoo keeper.

Dr Who

The Magic Roundabout, starring Florence, Zebedee and Dougal, 1966.

Edison Lighthouse – *Love Grows (Where My Rosemary Goes)* reached No. 1 in 1970.

Jackson 5 – *I Want You Back* reached No. 2 in 1970.

The Kinks – *Lola* reached No. 2 in 1970.

Mungo Jerry – *In the Summertime* reached No. 1 in 1970; *Baby Jump* reached No. 1 in 1971.

Smokey Robinson & The Miracles – *Tears of a Clown* reached No. 1 in 1970.

Dave Edmunds – *I Hear You Knocking* reached No. 1 in 1970.

Free – *All Right Now* reached No. 2 in 1970.

New Seekers – *I'd Like To Teach The World To Sing* reached No. 1 in 1971.

Gilbert O'Sullivan – *Underneath the Blanket Go* reached No. 1 in 1971; *Claire* reached No. 1 and *Ooh-Wakka-Doo-Wakka-Day* reached No. 8 in 1972.

Eric Clapton – *Layla* reached No. 7 in 1972.

Don McLean – *American Pie* reached No. 2 in 1971; *Vincent* reached No. 1 in 1972.

Rod Stewart – *Maggie May* reached No. 1 in 1971, *You Wear It Well* reached No. 1 in 1972.

Dawn – *Knock Three Times* reached No. 1 in 1971; *Tie A Yellow Ribbon Round the Old Oak Tree* reached No. 1 in 1973.

T–Rex – *Hot Love* and *Get it On* reached No. 1 in 1971; *Telegram Sam* and *Metal Guru* reached No. 1 in 1972.

Little Jimmy Osmond – *Long-haired Lover from Liverpool* reached No. 1 in 1972.

Lieutenant Pigeon – *Mouldy Old Dough* reached No. 1 in 1972.

Alice Cooper – *School's Out* reached No. 1 in 1972.

David Cassidy – *How Can I Be Sure* reached in No. 1 in 1972; *Puppy Song/Daydreamer* reached No. 1 in 1973.

Slade – *Take Me Bak 'Ome* and *Mama Weer All Crazee Now* reached No. 1 in 1972; *Cum On Feel The Noize, Merry Christmas Everyone* and *Skweeze Me Pleeze Me* reached No. 1 in 1973.

The Sweet – *Ballroom Blitz* reached No. 2 in 1973, *Blockbuster* reached No. 1 in 1973.

Gary Glitter – *I'm the Leader of the Gang (I Am)* and *I Love You Love Me Love* reached No. 1 in 1973.

Suzi Quatro – *Can the Can* reached No. 1 in 1973.

Can You Imagine Life Without...?

Popular Inventions In Your Lifetime

Pampers – First became available in 1961. There were disposable brands available in the fifties, but they were messy and not waterproof. By the late 1970s, the brand controlled 75 per cent of all disposable diapers in the US.

Video Recorder – Sony introduced the Betamax video player in 1975, while JVC launched their VHS cassette recorder in September 1976. JVC got other Japanese companies to join them producing only VHS compatible video recorders and thus began the standard. RCA in America also backed VHS over Betamax, thus vastly increasing the success of the product in the US. By 1985, VHS accounted for more than 80 per cent of the VCR sales in the world and it was becoming difficult for Betamax owners to find tapes, blank or pre-recorded in their format.

Walkman – Launched in the summer of 1979 by Sony. It was originally seen as a failure, as the idea was developed initially as a 'Pressman', a small stereo recording device for journalists. It was too small for a recording mechanism, however, and could only play back tapes. But by 1980, after the vital addition of the headphones, the 'Walkman' was the most popular tape machine ever.

Microwave Oven – First designed by US company Raytheon in 1946, but it only became available on the market in 1953 and was almost as large and heavy as a refrigerator. It was redesigned by the Japanese who made it smaller and cheaper, and was marketed by Sharp in 1966/7. In 1968, 30,000 were sold internationally; by 1985, 15 million had been sold. The slow build up of the microwave's popularity may have been due initially to poor marketing, but also to suspicion and set ways of cooking.

Rubber Gloves – First invented in 1952 for surgical and industrial use. The London Rubber Company launched the household rubber glove in 1961.

Computer – The idea of the first mechanical computer was conceived by Charles Babbage in 1835, but never went beyond the design stage. The first computer was built by Americans John Mauchley and John Eckert in 1946, and weighed 30 tons. The first word processor was devised by the IBM company in 1964, but was the size of a desk and had no screen.

Mobile Phones – First available in the seventies, based on an idea developed by the US Bell Telephone Laboratories in the forties; lack of technology held the idea up for 30 years.

Post-it Notes – Went on sale in the US in 1980, and in Europe in 1981. In 1983, sales totalled $45 million, and for a number of years increased at a reputed growth rate of 85 per cent.

A young Eric Clapton with John Mayall and the Blues Breakers in 1966.

Remastered version available on Deram (Cat No. 844 827-2)

Fit at Forty

Dr David Haslam

For many people, 40 is the big barrier – the moment when they can no longer kid themselves that they really are as young as they feel. The dread words 'middle-aged' are looming, although the best definition of 'middle age' has to be 'two years older than you are now'. Is the old phrase 'life begins at 40' sheer nonsense, or does it contain a nugget of truth?

In fact, the forties are an age of extraordinary variety. Some 40 year-olds are fit and dynamic, whilst others are sluggish and bored. Some have young children; others have young grandchildren. Some run marathons; others get out of breath looking for the TV remote control. It's up to you to choose which you'll be.

Your Changing Body

Prevention is always better than cure. In your forties you need to pay attention to those simple things that will keep you healthy during the years to come.

- Many women already have regular check-ups, but men often wait until they are ill. Both sexes should have their blood pressure checked at least once every couple of years. Women should be aware of any changes in their breasts, and should ensure that they have regular cervical smear tests, and men should regularly self-examine their testicles. If you don't know how, ask your GP.

- Your body weight will creep up if you don't keep physically active. There is no such thing as middle-age spread. It's simply an excuse: weight goes on when you take too much food and drink in, and don't do enough exercise to compensate. That's all.

- Exercise is more important than ever. This doesn't mean you have to immediately buy a lycra outfit and join a gym, but if possible try to get at least three 20-minute sessions of real exercise each week. Anything that raises a sweat will do – watching sport on the TV doesn't count!

- The most important thing you can do for your health is to stop smoking. Smoking can cause bronchitis, emphysema, heart disease, circulation problems, gangrene, cancer and death. To add insult to injury, 20 cigarettes a day costs well over £1,000 a year. Also, if you have a non-smoking partner, you may want to consider the effect that your smoking is having on their health. Talk to your doctor if you need help giving up.

- A small amount of alcohol is probably good for the heart, but the absolute maximum per week should be 28 units for men, and 21 for women. A unit is the equivalent of half a pint of beer, a single measure of spirits, or a glass of wine.

- Despite what you thought when you were a teenager, the over-forties should be having a fabulous sex life. If interest is waning, it's more likely to be boredom than hormones responsible for this. So don't

John Peel entertains the nation on Radio 1, in 1969.

allow your love life to drift into a habit. The prescription you need is imagination, time, sensitivity, and love.

- In women, the forties may be the time when her safe reproductive years will be coming to an end, and the menopause may start. Whilst this typically happens in the late forties, or early fifties, it can happen earlier. Typical signs are hot flushes, mood swings, vaginal dryness, and erratic periods. But despite all the stories and articles, for one third of women the menopause causes no problems at all; for one third it can be a nuisance; and for one third it causes significant symptoms. Problems are not inevitable.

Your Changing Emotions

Whether you feel middle-aged or not, the forties is the prime time for the mid-life crisis. This seems particularly to affect men, who suddenly panic when they realise that they are never going to achieve all their dreams, and that the younger guys in the office seem to be having all the fun. If this is happening to you, do one essential thing. If you have a partner, talk about it. Your partner isn't necessarily part of the problem, but can help with the solution.

Don't feel an obligation to try and fill every waking moment with activity. Take time out just to be. After all, as a psychologist once said, we are human beings, not human doings. Make sure you take time out to relax, by yourself, or with a partner; do things you enjoy; buy a relaxation tape; or invest in some aromatherapy oils.

If you don't simply feel stressed, but also feel constantly unhappy, with disturbed sleep, poor appetite, loss of interest and enthusiasm, and a reduced sex drive, then you could well be clinically depressed. This is very common, and very treatable. Talk to your doctor.

These days, few jobs are for life. Being made redundant in your forties is a traumatic blow, but it can be the beginning of fresh opportunities, a kick start out of the rut in which you may, unwittingly, have been. Many jobs now have short-term contracts, but this can be to your advantage. You may have 20 years of working life left, more than enough for almost every employer, and you also have experience: so sell yourself.

If you've got children, they may well be reaching the teenage years. The whole point of parenthood is for your children to become independent adults; and if they do, you worry. So save your concern for the things that really matter, not the trivialities that don't. Is that hair-style really worth getting angry about? After all, just think what you were like at their age. Let go of your children if you want to keep them.

By 40, you've had 20 years of adult working life and still have about the same to come before retirement. Now is the time to take a good look at what you are

Oz magazine, the voice of the seventies underground.

doing. Is this what you want? If it isn't, take action now. You've only got one life, and there's a lot of it still to live. Don't waste it. But do avoid panic behaviour. Selling everything, quitting your job, and heading for a Greek island may sound idyllic, but you really need to think about the practicalities.

More than anything else, however, now are the years when it really is worth keeping yourself physically fit. Nothing can be a better investment for the years to come, especially as turning 40 is more of a psychological than a physical barrier. Life may not begin at 40, but the forties can be years of fun and activity. It's up to you.

David Haslam is married with two children and has been a GP for 22 years. He is a Fellow of the Royal College of General Practitioners, and has written numerous books – the most recent being Stress Free Parenting. *He also writes a column for* Practical Parenting *magazine, and frequently broadcasts on health topics.*

Forty Eurovision Song Contest Winners

1998   *Diva*, by Dana International, Israel. UK came second with *Where Are You?* by Imaani.

1997   *Love Shine A Light*, by Katrina and the Waves, UK.

1996   *The Voice*, by Eimear Quinn, Ireland. UK came eighth with *Just A Little Bit*, by Gina G.

1995   *Nocturne*, by Secret Garden, Norway. UK came tenth with *Love City Groove*, by Love City Groove.

1994   *Rock 'n' Roll Kids*, by P. Harrington & C. McGettigan, Ireland. UK came tenth with *We Will Be Free (Lonely Symphony)*, by Frances Ruffelle.

1993   *In Your Eyes*, by Niamh Kavanagh, Ireland. UK came second with *Better The Devil You Know*, by Sonia.

1992   *Why Me?* by Linda Martin, Ireland. UK came second with *One Step Out Of Time*, by Michael Ball.

1991   *Fangad Av En Stormvind*, by Carola Sweden. UK came tenth with *A Message To Your Heart*, by Samantha Janus.

1990   *Insieme: 1992*, by Toto Cutugno, Italy. UK came sixth with *Give A Little Love Back To The World*, by Emma.

1989   *Rock Me*, by Riva, Yugoslavia. UK came second with *Why Do I Always Get It Wrong*, by Live Report

1988   *Ne Partez Pas Sans Moi*, by Celine Dion, Switzerland. UK came second with *Go*, by Scott Fitzgerald.

1987   *Hold Me Now*, by Johnny Logan, Ireland. UK came thirteenth with *Only The Light*, by Rikki.

1986   *J'Aime La Vie*, by Sandra Kim, Belgium. UK came seventh with *Runner in the Night*, by Ryder.

1985   *La Det Swinge*, by Bobbysocks, Norway. UK came fourth with *Love Is*, by Vikki Watson.

1984   *Diggi Loo-Diggi Ley*, by Herreys, Sweden. UK came seventh with *Love Games*, by Belle & the Devotions

1983   *Si La Vie Est Cadeau*, by Corinne Hermes, Luxembourg. UK came sixth with *I'm Never Giving Up*, by Sweet Dreams.

1982   *Ein Bisschen Frieden*, by Nicole, Germany. UK came seventh with *One Step Further*, by Bardo.

1981   *Making Your Mind Up*, by Bucks Fizz, UK.

1980   *What's Another Year?* by Johnny Logan, Ireland. UK came third with *Love Enough For Two*, by Prima Donna.

1979   *Hallelujah*, by Milk & Honey, Israel. UK came seventh with *Mary Ann*, by Black Lace.

1978   *A Ba Ni Bi*, by Yizhar Cohen & Alphabeta, Israel. UK came eleventh with *The Bad Old Days*, by Co-Co.

1977   *L'oiseau Et L'enfant*, by Marie Myriam, France. UK came
       second with *Rock Bottom*, by L. De Paul and M. Moran.
1976   *Save All Your Kisses For Me*, by Brotherhood of Man, UK.
1975   *Ding Ding Dong*, by Teach-in, Netherlands. UK came
       second with *Let Me Be The One*, by The Shadows.
1974   *Waterloo*, by ABBA, Sweden. UK came fourth with *Long
       Live Love*, by Olivia Newton-John.
1973   *Tu Te Reconnaitras*, by Anne-Marie David, Luxembourg.
       UK came third with *Power To All Our Friends*, by Cliff Richard.
1972   *Apres Toi*, by Vicky Leandros, Luxembourg. UK came sec-
       ond with *Beg, Steal Or Borrow*, by The New Seekers.
1971   *Un Banc, Un Arbre, Un Rue*, by Severine, Monaco. UK
       came fourth with *Jack in the Box*, by Clodagh Rodgers.
1970   *All Kinds of Everything*, by Dana, Ireland. UK came sec-
       ond with *Knock Knock Who's There?* by Mary Hopkin.
1969   *Boom Bang-A-Bang*, by Lulu, UK.
       De Troubadour, by Lennie Kuhr, Netherlands.
       Un Jour, Un Enfant, by Frida Boccara, France.
       Vivo Cantando, by Salome, Spain.
1968   *La La La*, by Massiel, Spain. UK came second with
       Congratulations, by Cliff Richard
1967   *Puppet on a String*, by Sandie Shaw, UK.
1966   *Merci Cherie*, by Udo Jurgens, Austria. UK came ninth
       with *A Man Without Love* by K. McKellar.
1965   *Poupee De Cire, Poupee De Son*, by France Gall, Luxembourg.
       UK came second with *I Belong* by Kathy Kirby
1964   *No Ho L'Eta*, by Gigliola Cinquetti, Italy. UK came second
       with *I Love the Little Things*, by Matt Monro.
1963   *Dansevise*, by Grethe & Jorgan Ingmann, Denmark. UK
       came fourth with *Say Wonderful Things*, by Ronnie
       Carroll.
1962   *Un Premier Amour*, Isabelle Aubret, France. UK came
       fourth with *Ring-a-ding Girl*, by Ronnie Carroll.
1961   *Nous Les Amoureux*, by Jean-Claude Pascal, Luxembourg.
       UK came second with *Are You Sure?* by the Allisons.
1960   *Tom Pillibi*, by Jacqueline Boyer, France. UK came second
       with *Looking High, High, High,* by Bryan Johnson.
1959   *Een Beetje*, by Teddy Scholten, Netherlands.
       UK came second with *Sing Little Birdie*, by Pearl Carr
       and Teddy Johnson.

Top Forty

Fame Comes to Those Who Wait

JFK became US president aged 43

•

Julius Caesar conquered Gaul aged 42

•

Christian Dior was 41 when he set up his own fashion house

•

Captain James Cook embarked on his voyage to Tahiti, New Zealand and Australia aged 41

•

Jacques Tati made his first film, *M. Hulot's Holiday* aged 45

•

René Descartes wrote his *Discourse on Method* aged 41

•

Muhammad received his first revelation aged 40

•

Harold Wilson became British Prime Minister in 1964 at the age of 48

•

Alexander Fleming discovered penicillin aged 47

•

George Foreman made a comeback to be the oldest world heavyweight champion aged 45, after 11 years off

•

J. R. R. Tolkein wrote *The Hobbit* aged 45

•

Frank Baum wrote *The Wizard of Oz* aged 44

•

Roger Moore became James Bond at the age of 44

•

Shirley Temple became UN Ambassador to Ghana at the age of 46, after a long career as an actress

•

Mother Theresa was 42 when she opened the Nirmal Hriday (Pure Heart) Home for Dying Destitutes in Calcutta, 1952

•

Dick Francis published his first novel aged 42

•

Kenneth Grahame was 40 when he wrote *The Wind in the Willows*

•

A. A. Milne was 42 when he wrote *When We Were Very Young,* which established him as a children's writer

•

Sir David Puttnam produced *Chariots of Fire* aged 40

•

Catherine Cookson wrote her first novel at the age of 44, and when she died aged 92, she had written 102

•

Paul Hogan was 47 when he starred in *Crocodile Dundee*, his first major movie success

•

Samuel Beckett was aged 46 when his play *Waiting For Godot* was first performed in Paris

Copyright Notices

Text
p.8, 9, 14, 15
> Statistics from *Social Trends*, Office for National Statistics, © Crown Copyright 1998.

Illustrations
p.3   *Dr No*, © United Artists, 1962. Photograph courtesy of the Kobal Collection.
p.6   © Tyne Tees Television, 1959. © Anglia Television.
p.10   © Mars Confectionary, 1960.
p.13   Barbie ® Doll, © Mattel Toys, 1958.
p.16   © Coca-Cola, 1960.
p.19   © Polydor, 1970.
p.23   © *News International*, 1962.
p.26   © Penguin Books, 1963. Illustration © Charles Raymond, 1963.
p.29   © Mercury Records, 1971.
p.33   © Oxford University Press, 1976. Illustration © Desmond Morris, 1976.
p.38   © BBC Television, 1965.
p.40   © BBC Television, 1966.
p.44   © Polygram International, 1966.
p.47   © BBC, 1969.
p.50   © Richard Neville.